THE UMPIRE'S BUNKHOUSE
Baseball Stories From Cooperstown's Dreams Park

Pals Forever!

Michael Marshall Brown

MICHAEL MARSHALL BROWN

The Umpire's Bunkhouse
Baseball Stories from Cooperstown's Dreams Park
All Rights Reserved.
Copyright © 2020 Michael Marshall Brown
v3.0

The opinions expressed in this manuscript are solely the opinions of the author and do not represent the opinions or thoughts of the publisher. The author has represented and warranted full ownership and/or legal right to publish all the materials in this book.

This book may not be reproduced, transmitted, or stored in whole or in part by any means, including graphic, electronic, or mechanical without the express written consent of the publisher except in the case of brief quotations embodied in critical articles and reviews.

Outskirts Press, Inc.
http://www.outskirtspress.com

ISBN: 978-1-9772-2431-6

Cover Photo © 2020 Michael Marshall Brown. All rights reserved - used with permission.

Outskirts Press and the "OP" logo are trademarks belonging to Outskirts Press, Inc.

PRINTED IN THE UNITED STATES OF AMERICA

COOPERSTOWN DREAMS PARK IS CLOSED FOR THE 2020 SEASON BECAUSE OF THE VIRUS

---∞---

This book is dedicated to my Dad

Special thanks
Noteworthy thanks to every one of the hundreds of umpires and to Linda Presutti and all her staff at Cooperstown's Dreams Park. Thank you to Lois Clermont, the retired editor of the Plattsburgh Press-Republican, NY, for her lifelong friendship and efforts to initially edit my book. Kudos to Nathan Weidner, a teacher at Canal Winchester High, for assistance editing photographs. Finally, to Alexandra Brown for taking the cover photo and her assistance in the making of "The Umpire's Bunkhouse."

The Umpires Bunkhouse

"The Umpire's Bunkhouse was written with heartfelt honesty about everything that goes on in Cooperstown. Cool book!
**Nate Siebert, Pennsylvania
Veteran CDP Umpire**

"Author Michael Brown's book underscores everything that is great about baseball. He's produced a wonderful behind-the-scenes look at umpires, doing what they do best for the love of the game."
**Mitch Stacy
Associated Press Writer
Columbus, OH**

"I have a strong sense of the author's love of the game of baseball and how Mr. Brown has sustained that love through umpiring. It's a fascinating book, one that I naturally read with great interest, but it will be a good read for anyone."
**Richard Long
Teacher at Kurn Hattin Homes, Vt.,
Umpire in Vermont**

"The Umpire's Bunkhouse is a compelling read, chock full of behind-the-scenes anecdotes and stories that stripped the mask of mystery off these men and women in blue. When I first donned an umpire's mask 25 years ago, I was told it is the only profession where you are expected to be perfect on Day 1, and then improve. Kudos to the author, Michael Brown, for letting the rest of the world in on the intrigue and the little-known world of the baseball umpire.
**Garry Harrington
Author, World Traveler,
College Umpire**

"It was interesting reading the lineup of varied characters. Terrific insight into the evolving sport of baseball. The Umpire's Bunkhouse will be an interesting read even for non-sports fans.

Lois Clermont
Journalist and Editor
Plattsburgh, New York

Table of Contents

Introduction i
1. My Story 1
2. The Issue at Hand 3
3. The Cooperstown Way 5
4. Ted Nugent and Jack 7
5. Dreams Park 8
6. Nate the Great 11
7. Papa Smurf 13
8. Grant the Great One 15
9. The Iron Horse 16
10. The Snoring Twins 17
11. The Hunters 20
12. Chin Music 22
13. The Players 23
14. The Fans! 25
15. Future Dreams in Cooperstown? 26
16. Really Big Bats 28
17. The Bully 30
18. The Heroes 32
19. Young Bucks 47
20. The Canadians 48
21. The Quiet Cowboy 49
22. Marketing Man 50
23. The Lonely Streets of Cooperstown 51
24. Gentleman Jim 52
25. Kelly 53
26. The Coaches 54
27. Uncle Charlie 55
28. Confidence Supreme 56

29. A Blast from the Past	57
30. A Homecoming	59
31. What do Umpires Talk About?	62
Conclusion	65

Introduction

Within a society of relatively decent souls, we are forever curious about solitary people behind the mask of the Lone Ranger or the Phantom of the Opera.

Or perhaps a secretive wild turkey hunter hunkered down in glorious springtime when everything is lush green, wearing nothing besides a camouflage mask and clothing.

The same is true for the incredibly beautiful sport of *baseball*. Men, and an expanding number of women, have the intestinal fortitude to crouch down, unflinching, behind home plate wearing an umpiring mask. They usually wear blue.

Who are those guys in blue? Who are they, really?

That's the objective of this book about the people who come from all over the nation to umpire in Cooperstown.

The intensity and core values of a man now gone, founder of Cooperstown Dreams Park, Lou Presutti, is the intrinsic and unspoken truth of what takes place each year in far upstate New York.

Linda Presutti retains a stately place of leadership in retaining the legacy of her husband.

Major League Baseball is in a period of angst. With major league firings of coaches in Houston, Boston and the New York Mets (and what is next?) there are no beating trash cans and cameras hidden away in CDP's outfield walls. No, not in Cooperstown.

It's pure baseball, and umpires are entrusted to help it endure.

With so much scorn poured down on umps across the nation from unruly fans, coaches and players, it is high time for revealing the naked truth about umpires.

Are they humans or robots? People in Cooperstown during the summer of 2019 overwhelmingly wanted to see a familiar human face behind the plate.

As Howard Taub explained during his first visit three seasons ago in Cooperstown as a coach, he found the baseball umpires to be mysterious. Their personalities were primarily shrouded in secrecy. Now after a week at the famed Dreams Park as an *umpire* during the summer of 2019, the Cleveland resident has discovered perceptions radically different.

"The umpires are very successful people, from all over the nation, like Kelly Allred who flies in from Utah. I think they come here because it gets them back in touch with their youth. We strive to be the best we can be," Taub says.

This book is a brave attempt at full disclosure; a look at the summer of 2019 and the adventures of several good folks.

1
My Story

IT IS A miracle and a sweet dream come true that I was able to umpire again at Dreams Park in Cooperstown.

On August 28 of 2018, I was admitted to Mt. Carmel East hospital in Columbus, Ohio. Eight days later, struggling for what little strength remained, I was released from the hospital after triple bypass, open heart surgery.

It scared me out of my mind and eroded my confidence as both a man and a baseball umpire. Realizing that being out cold and your heart laying on a table during surgery will do that to the bravest of men.

I had been working as an umpire at Dreams Park in late July 2018. Then back home in Ohio, a few weeks later, could not walk back to my car with my wife, Alexandra. We had been at a concert in downtown Canal Winchester, Ohio.

The signs were shortness of breath and difficulty walking without tightness in my chest. As my pal and high school baseball teammate Don Bruce in Vermont said, after my operation, I was fortunate to not drop dead at age 63 from a massive heart attack.

Initially flunking a stress test led to a hospital visit for a procedure that ideally would lead to a stint or two to alleviate the pressure. That was the best-case scenario but no such luck. Three of my arteries were completely blocked, the test abruptly ended, and triple bypass surgery was scheduled in three days.

The recovery was exhausting but helped along by a great surgeon, ICU nurses, and regular every-day nurses. My sister Karen Brown Ryan came up from North Carolina to help Alex take care of me.

Losing most all muscle tone, my weight dropped to 175 pounds and I was feeble. It was a humbling ride but with determination, slowly and surely, things got better.

God might have something to do with my recovery along with prayers from people all over the world.

Cooperstown would be a proving ground, umpiring about 10 to 12 games per week and more than 40 games in a month. *Plus staying in the bunkhouse!*

There was a high degree of anxiety. Would I be going home after the first week and unable to stand the frenetic pace. Or stiff and stone-cold in a wooden box!

But you can anticipate a happy ending to the rest of the story. When I got home from Cooperstown after a month, I felt much stronger, and my weight was up to 195 pounds.

One of the last things I did during a triumphant and learning experience was mail the treasured ring given by Dreams Park at the closing ceremony. It was postmarked from Cooperstown on Hall of Fame induction weekend to my Little League coach. He's 90 and lives in Florida.

He is Richard E. Brown and he is my Dad. This book is dedicated to his honor. I have loved baseball for 60 years because of Dad.

2
The Issue at Hand

FOR MORE THAN a century of baseball, a gaggle of fans have thought it is their undeniable right to verbally shout what should or should not be called balls and strikes.

That's baseball, you perhaps say. *That is absolutely ridiculous.* A coach, player or fan at 30 yards or more away, at extreme angles, erroneously think they can call a pitch?

In the age of Donald J. Trump, the issue has become more extreme, with players, coaches and fans frequently unleashing a scathing barrage against the umpires.

If the President can say anything he wants, why can't I? That's the general sentiment. Twitter and other forms of social media, without an editor or a fact check, make it worse.

More and more good umpires are quitting the sport, leaving schools and travel teams the unenviable position of scrambling to cover games.

National media is fanning the fire, also, challenging a veteran major league umpire for his strike and ball coverage during the October 2019 World Series between the Washington Nationals and the Houston Astros. Scrap the timeless situation of brave men, and some women, calling the pitches and the plays in favor of a robot?

Major League Commissioner Rob Manfred was widely quoted in 2019 about the usage of technology in the Arizona Fall League and the Atlantic League. Meanwhile, the view of all players, pitchers and hitters alike, was not good. Technology is not reliable, and strikes were called, even a pitch in the dirt.

Now, the new contract between major league umpires and the clubs call for, over the next five years, robot experimentation as umpires. Say it ain't so …

The overall consequences are grim for baseball.

In a sport, at least in my home state of Ohio, that has not raised the rate of pay in two years for umpiring high school games, and the last raise was **$2 per game**, how does any sane soul expect the scholastic leagues to pay for new technology like electronic robots?

The Fall Ball leagues in Arizona likely spent millions on podcasts, earphones, and other expensive electronic gear.

But beyond the technology, the ancient game of baseball faces a litany of other troubles.

The virus originating in China potentially cancels out all high school games as well as Cooperstown's fabled tournament.

Meager pay, no travel money, and added, extreme working conditions, are leading to the end of the sport as we have known baseball for 140 years. Unless …

Umpires are nice people behind the mask and there is a shortage of available umps.

Haven't you heard?

3
The Cooperstown Way

BASEBALL FANS WHO know the luster through a century and a half will understand the brand value of Cooperstown.

Whether you have been to the miniscule village before, or at least heard about its mystique, Cooperstown represents such a positive theme. Just saying the word emulates healing, soothing messages.

Maybe that's why I went back so soon despite my serious health issues.

It is home to the fabulous National Baseball Hall of Fame, and it has an uplifting way. The *Cooperstown way!*

There's something indeed unique about Cooperstown, the way you are greeted in a grocery store, the way local players - who grew up playing legendary Doubleday Field - speak with you. Their eyes sparkle and they have a sense of offering you a personal invitation to share the joy.

The *Umpire's Bunkhouse* is through the lens of an avid umpire. I have umpired 150 games per year for several consecutive seasons based in a little old, one stop light town. It's a suburb of Columbus, Ohio, one of the fastest growing cities in the nation.

Through the years I have been a championship Little League pitcher in Vermont, a college basketball player, a sports editor in Cooperstown and other New York State cities, and a state administrator for higher education in Ohio. I've worn many hats in a rapidly changing world.

I've had an enriched set of challenges and rewarding opportunities. Retired now, I am a book author, a substitute teacher, and an umpire. I also enjoy basketball officiating. All these part time jobs are opportunities most people don't want because of the difficulties and low pay. They are "give back" jobs that are rewarding to a tiny minority.

THE UMPIRE'S BUNKHOUSE

It is easier for most folks to complain about umpire's decisions on twitter or Facebook!

In Cooperstown, people give and ask for nothing in return. But the returns are so valuable; not in money, but in other subtle ways.

My umpiring story in famed Cooperstown includes overcoming a bully, and my rapid recovery from serious health problems, thanks to many friends.

It is a golden moment, albeit a small snippet in time.

Most of the games feature two-man umpiring crews, arguably the toughest demand on umpires. You just can't cover all the angles and all the field with two umpires. In the later rounds, in Cooperstown, three-man, and finally, in the championship game, six umpires are used just as they have every game for the major leagues.

Expectations for umpire performances in Cooperstown are very high.

First and foremost, like actor James Earl Jones' epic speech in the classic movie, "Field of Dreams," this book is written with an absolute love for baseball.

And it's the relationships that make it happen. It's the Cooperstown way!

4
Ted Nugent and Jack

AS A TESTIMONY to relationships, consider a random encounter. Ted Nugent – no, *not that* one – ran into me by chance in the bathhouse during our umpiring endeavors in Dreams Park.

Ted said he had a simple story for the book that might be of interest. He had just returned to Dreams Park after a brief journey. A small man with a big goatee and even larger heart, he went to pay his respects and honor Jack Francisco.

Jack was going to die soon from cancer.

He had been a popular mainstay of the weekly tournament's umpiring crews. Deep into his final days, Jack asked his friend, Nugent -- not the controversial rock star --about a hankering for a savored dessert. Well, that's all Nugent needed, and he went about gathering the ingredients and presented Jack with his favorite dessert.

Mr. Francisco was down to about 77 pounds prior to his death in early August of 2019. But he was eternally grateful to Nugent for his act of kindness.

As Ted, his real name is Tim, but nobody calls him that, told me the story, his eyes watered. "Jack Francisco was quite a guy, and a really good umpire. He was a dear friend," he admitted.

They had never met until seven years ago and had developed an amazing friendship over the years at Dreams Park. That relationship is typical of the men you will read about in the following chapters.

These baseball umpiring stories are about, and in tribute, to the Jack Francisco's all over the nation who come to Cooperstown.

5
Dreams Park

THE SETTING IS Dreams Park, a sprawling, private baseball nirvana about four miles south of Cooperstown.

It is a spectacular location in the verdant hills of Leatherstocking country of James Fennimore Cooper fame.

Once simply farm fields, since 1996, the 13-week schedule at the park is a dream come true for the founder and late Lou Presutti and his wife Linda. Lou passed suddenly in July of 2017 while Linda remains the heart and soul of the park.

It is believed to be a largest baseball tournament in the nation for youngsters.

Each week, 104 teams of 12-year-olds and their coaches come to the park of 22 manicured fields for a grueling tournament. It culminates in just two teams still alive for the championship game.

The finale is played in front of about 2,500 people in a major league stadium setting. They come from Hawaii, California, Florida and even Idaho.

Unlike the perceived, more famous Little League World series in Williamsport, Pa. the teams are not "town teams" but most often are heavily recruited "travel team" players for their maturity, height, and overall talent on the diamond.

Alumni from previous years includes guys you might have heard about; major league millionaires Mike Trout, Bryce Harper, and David Price.

Home runs are the highlight and the grand expectations of every game. The fences are all green monsters that are exactly 200 feet from the plate. Players are allowed any size and kind of bat they want.

They can haul a telephone pole to the plate, if they can swing it!

The first time I umpired in 2018 the first three batters were taller than me; that's five-foot-ten. All three sluggers consecutively hit the ball over the fence, and it was 34-0 after four innings!

Ka-Pow, pow, pow! The sound of metal bats is loud and proud in Cooperstown.

The teams play six games in pool play, from Sunday through Tuesday, then face a grueling elimination round on Wednesday and into Thursday. The final two teams play for a championship game complete with fireworks and a big crowd at the Little Majors Stadium. It's a classic setting complete with healthy doses of patriotism.

The 100 umpires each week come from every corner of the nation, sponsored by the visiting teams. They stay in eight, 12-man bunkhouses and it is like summer camp for kids. But the umpire age range is 21 to 80.

There is a natural bonding process depending what bunkhouse you stay in for a week. I was in bunkhouse 41A. The bunkhouses are crowded with double-decker metal beds with a thin mattress on the bottom level.

There is no air conditioning, no television, and the bathrooms are a hike for those of age. There's no heat, either, so June mornings are nippy. Why do these men keep coming back? *It is a beloved experiment in humanity.*

Umpires who do indeed have comfortable beds and a good life back home someplace, give it all up. Several of the men stay for the duration of 13 consecutive weeks. Why? For the love of baseball, the kids, their fellow umpires, and to be the best umpire they can be.

Rick Kalchuk is one of the tallest, loudest, and *most kind* of all the umpires. "It's like being in the (military) service. We sleep in bunkhouses, share shower rooms and the food sucks. But otherwise, it's a rewarding summer being here to umpire."

It doesn't hurt that the pinnacle of baseball – *The Cooperstown National Baseball Hall of Fame* – is just up the road in the beautiful hills of Leatherstocking country. All the umpires make the pilgrimage.

The story of baseball continues at a fabled pace, intertwined with magical humanity. At a time when umpires are yelled at more and more, it's time for revealing the truth.

THE UMPIRE'S BUNKHOUSE

The umpires are sweet, serious, and robust men.

A few weeks after working four weeks there in 2019, I was assigned to umpire a late summer league game back in Westerville, Ohio.

Before the game, I met John Fox, an electrician who was assigned to umpire the game with me. Immediately, I noticed the faded Dreams Park shirt on his back. He proceeded to tell me, with glee in his voice, many experiences in Cooperstown over the last few years.

He makes his own umpire pins for sharing and he treasures the memories. *That's the Cooperstown way!*

The stories are all common bonds of humanity. Black, white, brown, it does not matter what skin color. Mostly, most of us were red, from constant exposure to the sun!

Terry Vaughn is from Pittsburgh and now Orlando and we became instant pals forever. "Mr. Mike," was his pleasant way of addressing me. We talked mostly about umpiring but also the reality that your color of skin in Cooperstown means nothing. It is a matter of character.

It is how we call plays on the field, and how we manage the great game of baseball. Be prepared to laugh, cry, and wonder when you find out what it's like being an umpire at a high level.

The peak of emotions is centered accurately by umpire Doug Harvey, the ninth professional umpire to be inducted into the Baseball Hall of Fame a few years ago. He called umpires "the necessary evil" but also "the integrity of the game," in his induction speech.

"You have to be ready to do your best," he said, regardless of whether you slept in a fine hotel, your comfortable home, or a crowded bunkhouse the night before the game.

That's the Cooperstown way.

6
Nate the Great

A LITTLE GNOME of a man, with an enormous heart, Nate Siebert is the epitome of a Cooperstown umpire.

I find myself waking up early mornings in my comfortable home in Ohio and imagine forever the sound of Nate shuffling his feet from bunk to bunk in the crowded bunkhouse.

"Sheelunk, sheelunk, sheelunk!" Nate has delivered our laundry once again!

This involves pulling a wagon a quarter mile to the big tent, sorting through all the 100 umpires' neatly folded clothing, and then managing to return to bunkhouse 41A. Umpires are gifted with free laundry service.

Nate does this sort of thing at 6:30 am in the foggy, misty mornings of Cooperstown's summer season. Doesn't ask; doesn't expect money. He just does it at the crack of dawn most every day.

Meanwhile, he's a fine umpire regularly honored with the coveted task of working the final, championship game. That's considered the ultimate honor, to be selected to the umpiring crew for the final game.

Nate was working a July championship game in front of a huge crowd when he noticed something coming out from under the stands.

I was sitting near home plate with other umpires when suddenly there was a stampede of umpires, players and fans. It was a skunk! "I've never seen people run so fast," Nate said with a chuckle.

For Nate the great, there's the good life to enjoy, all centered on the kids who come to 41A bunkhouse to trade him colorful and meaningful pins. Nate's got them all from Hawaii, Vermont, and every place in between. He has somewhere around 20,000 pins, perhaps more!

THE UMPIRE'S BUNKHOUSE

"Mind your own business" played at least 100 times during our stay together, the classic Hank Williams song.

That tune is only 60 years-old! But it became our theme song, thanks to Nate's tape machine.

His personal story is remarkable. He's been coming to Dreams Park all summer, week after week of umpiring and pin trading, despite a series of physical ailments. He never complains and offers a shy grin when somebody makes good natured fun of his shakes and twitches.

"My father wasn't home much when I was young. But my mom had 22 kids," he recalls with a twinkle in his eye.

"One day when my father was home, I was nine then, my Dad came over to me and told me to sit in his lap," Siebert said in all seriousness.

"I heard you are a pretty good ballplayer," his father said. "Tomorrow, I'll come and see you play baseball for the first time."

Nate went to bed that night long ago with his heart bursting with pride. Two hours later, he was awoken by a brother. "Wake up, your father is downstairs. *He just died.*"

Baseball has literally been Nate's lifeblood. He lives in rural Pennsylvania and keeps in touch with many family members by phone.

Another highlight is his happy addiction to playing lottery tickets on his one day off. The local Stewart's store looks forward to Nate coming in on Friday, and he looks forward to walking away with a bunch of big bills.

7
Papa Smurf

HIS BED, IF you could call it that, was right next to my bunk in 41A.

He had a tarp covering the opening, blankets around the sides, and the bunk was piled high with candy, pins, and a look-alike Santa statue with a white beard in baseball gear.

James Seed really does look like Papa Smurf. The white beard, a twinkle in his eye, and always looking out for other smurfs.

Seed is all about the kids.

He's a big, exuberant kid, too. I'll never forget the sight of him, a Thursday night at the start of closing ceremonies, standing to greet each of the players (104 teams) marching toward the stadium.

It was hot, a really sweltering day for late July in Cooperstown. Beads were around his neck and he was grinning from ear to ear; his white beard glowed in the late afternoon light.

Seed offered encouragement, beads, or a high five. "Everything is for them, that is why we are here," he was always fond of saying.

But his cartoon character masks his day job. A man with deep connections with the United States Navy, he lives in Virginia. He has enriched experience managing teams of people and he's clever in maneuvers, especially in difficult circumstances. Papa Smurf helped coach me through some difficulties.

We are both in our early 60s. I enjoyed our private one on one conversations very much.

Another common bond is fishing. Although my forte is freshwater fishing, his great love is snook fishing in the ocean.

During our three weeks together, we shared much. The sounds of his radio going off at random times, his late night, sweet talks on the phone to his wife back in Virginia, were all treasured.

I was honored to be selected for a championship game assignment on July 25.

After a hard liner skimmed just foul down the line, and I signaled foul with both hands; a voice from the crowd was loud. "Hey, this isn't football season yet, *it's baseball ...* "

That was Papa Smurf! He and most of my 41A bunkmates came out for the championship game and sat near me to watch. It was an honor.

That is the kind of men they are. *The Cooperstown way.*

8
Grant the Great One

HE CAN SLEEP under any time of day and circumstance. But when he is awake, he's a dynamo.

Grant Hutchinson from Zanesville, Ohio is the primary reason I was in Cooperstown. His big laugh and engaging personality are well known at the park, almost like Jackie Gleason's character from old-time Honeymooners television.

"Awaaaay weeee goooo," Grant often elongates his words!

It all started in 2018 when he asked me during an umpire training session one snowy night in Columbus, Ohio, "Hey, you want to go to Cooperstown with me and umpire a big national tournament?"

Little did he know my experiences from 1979 to 1984 was serving as sports editor of the Daily Star in the Cooperstown-Oneonta region. That's when newspapers were king of all media.

Grant is a tremendous umpire, does college games around Ohio, and in an interesting kind of way, has become a mentor to me. He's more than 30 years younger.

In Cooperstown during the summer of 2018, I was working behind the plate with him. He was umpiring two-man in the field. He started a routine of pointing and I surely looked like a deer in the headlights. What in the name of Jesus did he mean? It was a first look at the way collegiate umpires communicate and rotate silently.

But my lasting memories of this sweet person is how much quieter our bunkhouse is when he's away or he's sleeping. He's a friendly force!

9
The Iron Horse

HARDLY BENT OVER, and no signs of old age setting in, Boddie Sullivan is the dean of umpires at the park.

The southern man is the Cal Ripken of Dreams Park and he claims to have umpired for 104 consecutive weeks over eight years. Call him the iron horse.

If you need to talk baseball, go find Boddie.

He stayed a few bunkhouses away from my base at 41A and has a deep appreciation for Dreams Park.

"I love the Park's magic and all the stories. Most people don't know that Dreams Park is the largest youth tournament of its kind in the entire world."

Boddie is very complimentary of Coach Lou, his father, and Linda Presutti. "They keep the dream alive."

Check all the rosters for the final day of competition, and Boddie's name is everywhere. He knows everyone. Everyone knows him.

"I don't remember all the names of the players and umpires of course, but the thousands of faces are all familiar to me. Several players are major leaguers now."

10
The Snoring Twins

SNORING IS A calamity in the 41A bunkhouse. The first night there, in late June, my bunk was between Ron Gill and Kevin Fields. Both men slept soundly.

I did not.

Unfortunately, they snored, that rumbling, deep down, erratic noise. Sounds like a freight train coming off the tracks.

It was so bad I got up from my bunk, groggy, grabbed my sleeping bag, and headed out to the parking lot to sleep in my car. It was frosty, cold and 2 a.m.

But there was a problem. All the park gates were locked, and I had to walk half a mile to the one that was open. The security guard was surprised to see me.

I got off to a rocky start with Ron and Kevin. But so much like the camaraderie of Cooperstown, we became pals forever.

Ron was on a landmark visit with personal considerations. From Florida now and originally Connecticut, he was once a star athlete. But now he was in a low place.

He had not umpired regularly in quite some time as he mourned the recent loss of his dear brother, Larry.

"We were close, real close. I did not stop crying for a long time," Ron said, his voice almost a whisper. In Cooperstown, this was his first foray into high level umpiring in quite some time, and he wasn't sure he could still do it the way he once did.

God and fate are amazing forces, and Ron got matched with me to umpire together. He shakily asked if I would switch with him, take the plate for the first game, because he wasn't sure he could do the job. Well the miraculous story ends by the end of the week with him getting all his superb skills back. We were a dynamic team.

Off the field, by the end of the week, we were in-separable and he often introduced me as John McCain, because of my resemblance to the late Senator that I have experienced many times in the past.

We were both good friends with Kelly Allred from Utah, who was only in Cooperstown for a week, and we gave council and many words of encouragement to each other.

There was nothing we wouldn't talk about and though we had just met a week before, it was like Allred and Gill were pals forever.

Kevin Fields stands six-four and 235 pounds, and you'd never know in real life he likes growing dainty flowers in his garden outside Jacksonville, Fla. He retired in September 2019 as a mail carrier.

But his sweet southern drawl and his storytelling are exceptional. He told me incredible stories involving his baseball life. We laughed and cried.

During one occasion, he was umpiring, his big body stooped low behind the plate, and the catcher suddenly delivered a very loud fart just before the pitch was thrown. The batter quickly stepped out of the box with his face all twisted. There was an awkward silence.

"All I could think to say to them," he said slowly, "was it is clear to me, the plate needs to be brushed off," Fields said with a grin.

We joked all the time. The topic came around to movies and we both loved George Clooney in "Oh Brother, Where Art Thou." Clooney and his buddies said somebody who did something admirable was "bona-fide."

Well, when Kevin found out a few weeks later that I had made the championship game, he said in his southern drawl, "You know what, now that you've made the championship game, you are absolutely "Bone-aaaaa-Fiiiiide."

Fields adored his father and remembers watching live television with his Dad when Jack Ruby killed Lee Harvey Oswald after the trauma of John F. Kennedy's assassination in Dallas.

That was a long time ago, in 1963.

"He died 25 years ago from cancer of the lungs and that taught me to quit smoking," Fields said of his father.

THE SNORING TWINS

When he was young, the Florida native played on the Picketsville Civic Club.

"The kids in the league used to pick on the PCC team. They didn't know how to spell much of anything, and they thought that PCC meant Picketsville **Sewer** Club."

"They couldn't spell *civic*." Those of us listening in the bunkhouse to this story roared with laughter.

A month after having a grand time together in Cooperstown, he sent me a package from Florida to Ohio. It was a photograph, in black and white, of the PCC Little League team, circa 1964.

He's the bat boy in the photo of boys with knee-high socks, PCC letters on their chests, and his Dad is head coach standing on the left. It was more than 50 years ago!

"Thanks for writing a book about all the experiences in the bunkhouse," he said to me in a handwritten note.

"Notice in the photo, the socks are just like the boys today at Cooperstown Dreams Park. The memories of those days are the main reason I enjoy the trip to CDP each summer."

His classic photo stirs my own regal memories. The 1960s. The Rotary club; coached by my Dad in Bellows Falls, Vermont.

There's a team photo in my office now from 1961 when my late brother Peter and I were little batboys. The complete set of team photos from Vermont, all in black and white, shows substantial growth of all the players over four years.

In 1967, I was the undefeated pitcher tossing a no-hitter in the championship game. We treasured it all.

But at dinner back home in late July of 1967, my father made a comment that has haunted me since. "If you were a better hitter, we would have won the championship by more than 2 to nothing."

Kevin's favorite baseball glove when he was a kid was special. "I really did love that glove. But I left it outside the house one night, and my dog chewed it up."

11
The Hunters

DON GORDON, JOHN Boss and Ralph Diaz are some of the last of a special breed of Americans known as admirable, skilled hunters of the whitetail deer.

It is as if James Fennimore Cooper's *Last of the Mohicans*, comes alive when you talk with Mr. Gordon. He was in our bunkhouse for a week and we became close.

One evening Gordon and I were strolling back from dinner under the big tent, with fellow hunter Boss, from New Jersey, and the sun was setting behind us.

Lo and behold, I got this crazy idea, looking at our three shadows, and put both hands up like a big, antlered buck deer.

Don, who is nearing 70 but strong and tall, caught on quickly and put his huge paws and his long arms in the air.

John, about a foot shorter than Don, followed suit and we were three mature bucks -- our shadows at least -- prancing down the blacktop past the players' bunkhouses.

We were all grinning from ear to ear.

I just wonder what the boys from Hawaii and Chicago were thinking if they caught a glimpse of three old-time umpires laughing and prancing.

Don is from northern Michigan and we shared many stories about the legend and lore of deer hunting. He hunted the way I once did in Vermont, on the ground all day, rifle in hand, trying to outsmart wily deer.

A common theme that we agreed on is that umpires and deer hunters have much in common. We are alert and aware of sudden, unexpected things happening at the strangest of times.

THE HUNTERS

Slowly but surely Don became more and more amiable. The big man lost his long-time career building Buick automobiles in Michigan several years ago. We talked freely about the ups and downs of life. That's hard for many men.

John Boss is a great contrast in size and personality to Don, but he shares so much. He grew up a tough guy in Jersey and he regularly killed deer for the meat it would serve his family.

John is a handyman supreme and he was often called on in the bunkhouse to fix something. He's a "helper."

On top of that, he is truly a friend who will do anything to help. That's a gift that most umpires treasure.

Ralph Diaz is complex and interesting at all levels. He's a deer hunter, too, and travels all parts of the country.

Now retired, the native of Miami, FL is now living near the Tennessee and Georgia line. He's a great umpire and mentor and is frequently selected to work the final rounds of the weekly tournament.

Ralph is arguably the best umpire in Cooperstown, and each spring he's assigned to work college games.

Boddie Sullivan, Albert Juarez and Kelly Allred will get some votes for best umpire of all the crews in Cooperstown, but my money is on Diaz.

Diaz travels during the fall months and is coming to my new home to hunt the big whitetails of Ohio. It's hard to imagine him covered in camo from head to toe.

His eyes grew wide when he sat with me and listened to tall but true stories of towering tines that live secluded near my house.

A stand is all set up, 12 feet up a tree, in a secret spot, for Diaz in full camo to bow hunt in the autumn.

12
Chin Music

THE FIRST FRIEND of early summer was a newcomer to the bunkhouse from Cleveland named Howard Taub.

He has a brilliant and encyclopedic mind. His dear wife is from Israel and she was once in the army. His talents and experiences have taken him overseas to Israel and to the Caribbean. Asked about the magic of certain old-time baseball words, like chin music, he said, "I'll look it up" he said in reference to always ready phone. "Hey, I got it, it says a way of pitching. Don Drysdale would often throw a high and hard one. Chin music."

But don't plan on winning an argument with him on anything to do with his beloved Cleveland Browns. He made a bet with me the Browns would be dramatically improved and be in the AFC title game. Alas, in 2019 they did not make the playoffs and again fired their coach.

He had the middle bunk, the worst possible location because everybody had to walk past his space. But he never complained, and I don't know how he slept.

Howard went with me when we toured Cooperstown and did a walk-through and a remember when of the lavish Otesaga Resort Hotel on the shores of the big lake.

I showed him the spectacular ballroom where the Hall of Famers, old and new, come to the Otesaga each summer. My memories of the early 1980s as sports editor of the Daily Star were sharp as I told him about meeting face to face the big stars of the game. Warren Spahn, Al Kaline, Hank Aaron, Frank Robinson and Cool Papa Bell all told me great stories.

But Howard's eyes really came alive when I talked about spending a night watching the Oneonta Yankees with the famous Cleveland legend, Bob Feller. Bob was his favorite.

13
The Players

THE ONLINE CHATTER before the tournaments, mostly from the moms, was centered on how much time would they get to spend with their sons, and who would make their beds and cook for them.

That all changed in a week. *A week.* Boys became independent, fine young men. They weren't allowed their cell phones, manners were required, and they respected the umps.

So many fine players; they dress in simple uniforms, with no names, red for home and blue for away.

The size of the players is staggering with the better teams frequently having several sluggers nearly six-foot. They are 12 years old? Check those birth certificates.

There was a tiny catcher behind the plate one game that I worked as an umpire, and he was gutsy, quick and had a great attitude.

After the game, I presented him my Dreams Park plate brush and posed for a photo. He'll remember that game.

The Hawaii team who got thumped by a team from St. Louis was unforgettable. After the game, both teams gathered in left field and the Hawai team did a traditional island dance. It made us remember why the game is played.

Major leaguer Matt Carpenter of the St. Louis Cardinals was at the game (he sponsors the team) and we spoke briefly and stood there as one, major leaguer and umpire, admiring the players celebrating in the outfield.

Another Hawaiian team won a game, and by tradition, called the two of us umpires back on the field and presented us with several gifts from the islands.

There was a man child who was like Babe Ruth's legend. We all

THE UMPIRE'S BUNKHOUSE

knew he was going to hit a homer. He hit three that day despite pitchers trying to pitch around him.

Relationships with coaches were intensified when I worked the field. Everything is close, the coach right next to you by first base, and hundreds of fans behind you.

A New York team was involved with a player in a rundown between first and second and it lasted for 10 throws. I ran like a gazelle, well sort of, to stay ahead of that play.

The first base coach smiled and said they would have a team reunion 20 years from now, invite me, and show that amazing rundown on video.

It wasn't always a happy moment for one of the teams. In one of the final games, I was working at third base and the catcher rifled a throw toward the base. The third basemen took the snap throw and got the runner out by inches.

My windmill out call was emphatic and you should have seen the stare I got from the base coach. But there was no argument.

Cooper Janowicz was the best hitter at that age I have ever witnessed. He hit 16 home runs *during the week* and was from the Michigan team that sponsored me.

Some of the umpires work to make the games end quickly. The better umpires, including me, not in an arrogant way, want games to last and be memorable competitions.

The boys will enjoy and remember the games, not for the score, but for the style of play, long after they leave Cooperstown.

14
The Fans!

THERE ARE THOUSANDS of parents, grandparents and well-wishers at the tournaments each week.

Did any of them holler at the umpires? Not many did but security came by a few times in the later games with so much at stake. The majority were sweet.

One day I was heading back to my car between games and I ran into a Dad, Mom and their daughter, a young girl named Brooklynn.

Dad is Joe Chow and his wife is Lisa and they live about 30 miles south of San Francisco. They were rooting for their son Ashton and his teammates from California.

We easily struck up a warm, sweet conversation. They offered a pin and I did not have one but said I was working on Field 20 in the morning. Well, my game the next morning ended early, a mercy rule, and I missed them. Brooklynn, as it turned out, went around asking for me.

When we finally met up, it was a magic moment. I brought a plate brush, and an umpire pin, and we posed for a family photo with a baseball signed "Pals Forever."

Four different teams sponsored me and one of the grandparents of the team from Pittsburgh said games reminded him of the character of Forrest Gump. "You never know what you're going to get from 12-year-old kids," he said.

Pittsburgh, two teams from Michigan, and one from North Carolina were great sponsorship teams. Each team is required to sponsor an umpire for the week.

Andi Janowicz befriended me when her son Cooper's Michigan team came to compete. She was soft-spoken and so kind, not a typical "Little League Mom." She was the mom of Cooper, the best all-around player you can imagine.

15
Future Dreams in Cooperstown?

WE MET BY chance one morning at the breakfast tent. As it turns out, Ken Godnavec said he was into politics, and we share interests in this arena.

Half an hour after first meeting, we walked out of the tent knowing very likely we would work together on a future campaign. First the legislature, next the Governor's seat. Ken and I are both from Ohio.

Ken looks like a cross between a mountain man, and a shrewd, wise soul who could be a college professor. His beard is a little on the gray side, and he's proud to show he's got a full head of hair.

Mr. Americana Man. That's what I called him and that's what his platform might be in Ohio. Stay tuned. Governor Godnavec, are you ready to run?

There are other umpires who would be dynamite political leaders. Jim Wergzyn, know affectionally as "Rollie" because of his neat, handlebar mustache – like Hall of Fame pitcher Rollie Fingers -- plays music and can charm anyone.

Rollie was selected for the finals on the final week of the season in late August. His pride in the position and for the entire summer, was unmistakable. His facebook post depicting an empty bunk said it all, "breaking camp, a great summer."

Andy Joyner is from New Jersey and for entertainment during games, he routinely threw the ball out of the park from his plate position. He's got style and he pitched in college.

Dustin Warman is a southerner I worked with, and he posed for a great photo before the game. The skilled photographer was a coach! Dustin loves fishing and went to my favorite spots from long ago, Glimmerglass State Park.

FUTURE DREAMS IN COOPERSTOWN?

Kevin Davis borrowed a light blue umpiring shirt from me, gave it back, and is a pal forever.

The championship game umpires were the tallest ever selected. I was the short man at five-foot-ten. Plate umpire Todd Johnston, first basemen Dom Machado and right field umpire Dwayne Smith were all between six-four and six-nine. Derek Ivinski and Joe Wynn were both six-feet tall.

Wynn is a character from Louisiana and loves to duck hunt. Plate ump Johnston is from Atlanta, and Smith can still play high level hoops at six-foot-six.

Ray Smith is a city boy from Chicago, and he hung out with me and we shared rides to the grocery store. He'll be back year after year.

The future of umpiring at Dreams Park, unless management changes the bunkhouse arrangements, is epitomized by umpire Bill Hughes. He was only there during the day, changing clothes, talking shop, in the bunkhouse for a short time.

He slept in better conditions outside of the park. We can only hope and dream?

That is the beautiful thing about Dreams Park. It's not just the players who dream big dreams.

16
Really Big Bats

EVERY LEAGUE IN America, including the high school associations and the Cape Cod Wood Bat League, restricts the size and weight of bats.

Why is Dreams Park in Cooperstown, with its unrestricted bat sizes, so different?

I'm not one to criticize the great and late Lou Presutti but here's a thought. When he brilliantly imagined the park nearly 25 years ago, he saw the home run as something every kid, every parent, and fan justifiably wanted to see.

That's why the eight-foot-tall fences are 200 feet away from the plate. That's why kids who are five-foot-three and 90-pounds hit them out each game on basically pop ups. That's why six-foot-two kids hit them out with often the ball zooming out at least to 300 feet.

Did Lou Presutti see the day coming when the better teams have players, at age 12, about six-feet tall? *I don't think so.* Some would say blame it on the food and milk laced with human growth hormones.

Most of us in the 1960s who played baseball were between five-five and five-eight when we played.

The downside of the big bats? Kids get hurt, nearly every game. Shortstops get broken arms on two hoppers in the infield, and pitchers miraculously don't get killed by balls hit hard.

Tom Delaney, an umpire from Kansas, said we are not in Kansas anymore, Dorothy. He noted how many pitchers got shattered kneecaps and the like from batted pitches.

"Cooperstown is wide open on what bats the kids use, but all other leagues are restricting the size. Something is not right with this," the senior human resources official said.

How about wooden bats? That would add to the nostalgia.

REALLY BIG BATS

A calm and collected man, he did not think much of Cooperstown's Dreams Park when he arrived. But before the end of the first week and it was time to fly back to Kansas, he changed his story. "I'll be back again, that's for sure."

I overheard him saying he was going to have free time before boarding a plane in Albany. So, it was suggested Jack's Oyster House in downtown Albany, a place forever linked to politics in the state capital that I know well.

He later called me from Kansas to say the restaurant was fantastic.

17
The Bully

A NAMELESS SOUL, he is truly a very good umpire from the Washington, D.C. area. But his personality is like Jekyll and Hyde.

My first glimpse into how his personality changes on the field came in the second week. We were selected to a four-man crew the final day. I was at first base and he was the home plate umpire.

He called me in to home plate and growled at me to go and stop the excited fans from beating on the wooden walls during the intense game. "Go out there now!" he said in an irritated manner. *What's this all about, I thought to myself.*

But the dirt hit the fan the next week when he was selected as my crew chief.

This man turned the already difficult experience into a nightmare. He so unnerved me that as each inning went on, he second-guessed every move I made.

Toward the end of the week, he said things like "How old are you?" and really alarming, "Just starting out in baseball umpiring?"

One game started out with me umpiring at the plate and the bully in the field. This was *my* plate meeting and barely two minutes into the greetings with the two coaches, the bully said it's time to play ball, ended the meeting, and walked away. The two head coaches and I stood, quietly, in disbelief.

He got to me. It was the low point of Cooperstown. The essence of the issue is the short field in Little League, and when a hitter hit a screaming line drive to the outfield, he thought I was "going out."

I never left the dirt of the infield, but did turn my back to watch closely, especially the times a right fielder hurled the ball back in, trying to get the runner at first.

THE BULLY

I would turn to look at this umpire who had sprinted to second base. He said, "you're making me run!"

He did not recommend me, and I did not get an assignment, to work the final day of playoffs.

Meanwhile, there was a former major league umpire on his crew named John Lindsey from the state of Washington and I was looking forward to learning from him.

But he switched with me at the last minute and I had the plate. In the fourth inning, Lindsay called time and came down to the plate to say my strike zone is "more like college level" and urged me to open my zone.

The plate is 17 inches? Or, is it 24 inches?

In contrast, the very next week, I did a game at the plate and a fellow umpire from Miami Beach said my strike zone was superb. His son was the starting pitcher and umpire Carlos Lopez was watching from the parents' box.

As he signed a baseball, he said the best thing about my umpiring is "the Cuban women from Miami did not holler about *anything* you called ... that's really *gooooood*."

18
The Heroes

THERE WERE MULTIPLE heroes involved in quickly bringing me out of my umpiring funk.

I talked about the difficult crew chief with 41A bunkmates Papa Smurf, John Boss and Nate Siebert. They suggested I go and see Todd Sloka, head of the umpires along with John Carr.

Nervously, I did see Todd the first week of the "new" season and he was open to me. I started off telling him what a great place it was, and a grand experience. Then I told him about the bully.

He said it is sometimes a problem having umpires from all over the nation, because they do things differently in Ohio compared to Washington, DC.

Todd admirably earned his keep later with me when he took time to work with me and showed me how umpiring is a game "like a dance." He really encouraged me.

There are other people who helped me quickly turn around my craft. Greg Mattioli, a seasoned assigner from Coatesville, PA, was in our bunkhouse and helped me immeasurably. He was selected to work the plate for the championship game after the final week.

Dan Miller, the plate umpire for an early finals game who I greatly admired, gave me tremendous encouragement.

So did Phil Dumenil from Maryland, an astute political man, who noted my long face one day and took the time to inspire me.

The biggest turn-around point from a difficult week for me was in the fourth week. The first action was being selected to be the "rabbit" covering both the outfield and second base by veteran home plate umpire Gerald O'Dette from Florida.

"Got to have somebody who is calm and confident out there," O'Dette, a former Marine, barked out to me.

THE HEROES

It worked like a charm despite my limited experience in four-man umpire teams. We got the calls right in a tense, high-talent battle between two teams from Florida. My confidence soared.

The next week my crew chief was a California man named Albert Juarez. His brother Robert, a twin, is also a fine umpire, and they both have many years of experience at Dreams Park.

Albert was all business and he immediately assigned me to work the plate for two consecutive games while he took the infield. He watched me closely.

Juarez is a man who inspires confidence, and I thrived under his leadership. After the second game, he was all smiles and gave me a high five as we walked off the field. "Way to go, mis amigo," he said.

Rain fouled up the schedule and that caused me to take on four games per day, for two consecutive days.

After Wednesday's fourth game ended way late, I was really fatigued. I stumbled back to our 41A bunkhouse and went to see the roster of umpires honored by selection.

The roster was taped on the wall.

Quietly I scanned the list and noted early on my name was not in the first round or the second-round playoff games. Looks like I did not make it.

I kept on reading ... no elite eight, no final four ... then my spirits rose to unexplainable heights. My name was last on the list, selected for the championship game crew.

Turning around, my bunkmates were all smiles as they greeted me. I made the finals!

After closing ceremonies, we were hand-delivered our commemorative Cooperstown rings and were greeted warmly by Linda Presutti, head of operations Jeff Davis, Sloka, and Carr.

We came back as a championship umpiring crew for the final game escorted on a golf cart.

We lined up as one across the plate, and both teams were on the base paths. We introduced ourselves as did the players. All of this

THE UMPIRE'S BUNKHOUSE

was on live television and I later ordered a copy of the videotape. We stood in honor of the patriotic fireworks.

I shed some tears.

My mind was all over the place, thinking of many other places of honor during my public relations career and my newspaper career like the Windows on the World Restaurant in New York City's Twin Towers or a national convention in Austin, TX.

But none was like this in Cooperstown.

The game was won 8-0 by Beaver Valley from near Pittsburgh and I got to call three homers out of the park. The roar of the crowd.

Happy men resting and sharing friendship before a game at the bunkhouse.

Ron Gill and Michael Brown preparing for a two-man umpiring game.

The Little Majors Park ready for opening ceremonies.

Long-time CDP umpires Rick Kalchuk (shirtless) and Papa Smurf.

A team from Michigan and the winning team from Georgia kneel down together, giving thanks.

The St. Louis team and the Hawaii team celebrate together in the outfield.

Ken Fanti cleans up outside of Bunkhouse 41A.

Nate Siebert is king of pin trading with players.

The War Dawgs from Michigan, with really tall players, poses with the author.

The Norm Chow family had a warm greeting with the author.

Safe or out? The author closely looking at a tight play at third.
It was a pickoff play. The runner was out!

Ken Fanti, Papa Smurf, Ralph Diaz and dozing off, Nate Siebert, relax in front of the bunkhouse.

The author getting ready to call a pitch.

Selected for the final championship game, the tallest lineup ever, poses just before the big game. From left is Derek Ivinski, Joey Wynn, Todd Johnston, Dwayne Smith, Michael Brown, and Dom Machado.

Ah, the memories! Kevin Fields in front of his bunk, and his 1961 PCC Little League team. He's the batboy second from the right and his father is at the top left. Also, the 1966 Bellows Falls, Vt. Rotary Club. My father is at the top right and the author is third from the left.

Working the outfield for the championship game.

Actor Donald Sutherland takes a break with his makeup lady inside Cooperstown's Doubleday Field, circa 1980. That's Jim Curtis in the background. (Photo by M. Brown)

On stage of the annual Hall of Fame Ceremonies in 1980, the Splendid Splinter, Ted Williams, shares a personal moment with Jean Yawkey. (Photo by M. Brown)

19
Young Bucks

THERE IS A changing of the guard coming fast, and the average age of the umpires nationally is about 58.

Paul Hess and Matt Dykstra are part of the new wave and they are already accomplished umpires. Hess is 21 and he was a tall, talented player at the Park a few years ago.

Dykstra was fun to be around, sharing the same bunkhouse. From the Chicago area, he was a wise guy who made us all laugh. His new wife and baby at home keep him busy.

Wayne Litwiller from Missouri and A.J. Franzen from the St. Louis area were standout umpires.

All were drawn to Dreams Park by the vaunted Cooperstown name.

Litwiller lost his wallet and all his bunkmates in 41A were looking everywhere. He finally found it, covered up by clothing. That was a relief!

Papa Smurf nicknamed Franzen because of his resemblance to the lion from the *Wizard of Oz*, saying "put em up, put emmm uppppp."

We laughed each time.

20
The Canadians

LAST YEAR BRYAN Haskell was in my bunkhouse and he was an interesting character from near Toronto.

During the summer of 2019, he came to pick me up for an assigned game and bunkmate John Boss shouted out, "there is a seven-foot-tall Canadian here to see Mike Brown."

He wasn't quite seven- foot- tall.

We worked a tense game, he behind the plate and me in the field, and he was taking some grief from the coaches on his ball and strike calls. Suddenly, he called time and signaled he wanted to talk to me.

I hustled in and did not say a word.

"These coaches are driving me crazy with their chippy- ness, and I just had to talk to somebody … that's it, thanks for listening, and you can go back to your position now."

I just gave him a huge grin. Completely understood!

Richard Elmes is a fine gentleman from Guelph, Ontario and we did not get to spend enough time together. His birthday was the same week he umpired.

Soft-spoken and confident, as an umpire, he was just like that as a person. It was very agreeable, and he was always quick to say the right thing. Elmes posted on Facebook that at the end of August 2019 he had umpired 100 games at home near Toronto.

Elmes, as much as any of the umpires, recognizes the pleasure and the pain of the difficult task of umpiring.

I got to carry the Canadian flag in their honor at the closing ceremonies after they left early. Next summer, my friends.

21
The Quiet Cowboy

ROBERT STOUDT IS quietly the mainstay of Dreams Park bunkhouse 41A. He likes his naps and that's not easy in a crowded, usually sweaty, bunkhouse.

A tough man with tremendous endurance, at over age 60, he loved taking time to show me many photos of his carpentry and plumbing work.

But best yet were his photos of cattle and the bulls that are part of his family's rodeo in rural Pennsylvania.

"A lot of guys come in there nervous, and the cows and bulls know it. The guys get kicked. Now I just know where to touch them, and they go whereever I want them to go."

He organized and cooked for the crew at beautiful Five Mile State Park located right on Lake Otsego. It was our one day off at the beautiful lake where you can see a quarter on the bottom at 20 feet. The lake is clear, deep and chilly.

Bob drove a bunch of us to a weekend breakfast fly-in at a local, grass airport. He even took guys to his farm on the one day off the umpires get each week. He's that kind of guy.

Along the way, he's a steady umpire who is selected week after week for working on Thursday.

One thing you don't want to do is wake up Mr. Stoudt when he's taking a midday nap. Oh, my, the forlorn soul who gets too loud and wakes him up ...

22
Marketing Man

KEN FANTI IS the sort of man I seem to think worked with me in the past. He's got a brilliant marketing mind.

During one of many conversations, he held up a blue Dreams Park umpire water cup. "I can't manufacture the cup; I'll find some company to do that. But I could take it a long way in making it more of an attractive keepsake."

He's got a sharp mind. Hard of hearing, he's shrewd at deciding what he wants to hear in some conversations.

On the last day of my summer in Cooperstown, he presented me with a gift. It was a book called "The Quotable Hunter" by Peter Fiduccia and Jay Cassell. Ken signed it to, "Mike … To a Great Ump … A Great friend, Ken, Cooperstown, 2019."

I read that book at soon as possible when I returned to Ohio. Ken did not know that I knew Fiduccia from my time in New York as an outdoor columnist. His book is a treasured gift from a special friend.

A longtime marketing man, Ken calls home Chicago and Florida. I shared many meals with him and noted with respect his way of selling things and taking care of his friends.

23
The Lonely Streets of Cooperstown

IT'S HARD TO believe, but the home of the National Baseball Hall of Fame still only has one stoplight in town.

Kevin Gray, from Florida and New Jersey, walked the streets late at night with me and experienced a different life. The streets of gift shops, and the memorable Hall of Fame, the post office, the restaurants, were all closed.

It was eerie.

Gray and I visited late nights pubs to wind down when we umpired late games.

Even though the Hall of Fame induction ceremonies were coming up, at midnight the only noticeable change was main street was blocked. The street was deserted.

One warm night coming back to Dreams Park, with Gray, I wore flip-flops and they kept falling off. So, I said the heck with them, and walked barefoot through the quiet park.

"Are you nuts, do you know what people spit, spill and put on this pavement?" Gray said in is Asbury Park, NJ accent.

"You're wearing those weird pajamas (my shorts with pineapples) and if security stops us, and you are also barefoot, we're in big trouble," he said, a big grin on his face.

Get the entire experience, I say.

24
Gentleman Jim

JIM SERTON, MY gentleman friend from the New York City area, is a terrific guy.

We didn't start out all that well, because my head was on the pillow facing his bunk and he loudly opened a cooler the very first, early morning.

You know what that sounds like? A crunch of ice, the squeak of the cooler opening, and then closing; it's loud. But that was the last harsh times with Jim. I moved my pillow to the other side of the bed, and we became Pals Forever.

I was umpiring in the field in front of a big crowd one day and a fan offered me a fabled pin. Not carrying our umpire pins, I was about to say we would meet up later. But out stepped a tall, distinguished man with the NY accent, with a pin for me to give to the man.

It was gentleman Jim. He was observing the team that sponsored him and just happened to be there on the field I was working.

Later, he assigned me to cover first base in his four-man crew and the game was successful. I made 12 put-out plays and some were bang-bang.

You might have noticed I haven't been mentioning who played and what was the score ... contrary to many fan's awareness, umpires don't keep track of the score and don't favor any team. We call one play at a time.

He contacted me a few weeks after our time in Cooperstown to say he was going to the U.S. Open Tennis Championship game with his wife.

Now retired, Jim lives in Florida but calls New York his hometown area. I miss him.

25
Kelly

KELLY ALLRED FROM Utah was the first good friend I met at the Park in 2018, and his bunk was right next to mine during my initial experiences.

I will never forget him.

There are no coincidences in this awe-inspiring world and there was no chance occurrence that Kelly was next to me.

He is a Morman and is soft-spoken, good looking, and appears 30 years-old, while he is much older; he loves talking about his daughter getting married.

Kelly umps college games out west and is meticulous in his preparation. In contrast, the first year, I had three umpiring shirts to choose from. Kelly had about 15 all neatly dry cleaned and hung up on a rack.

His shoes were immaculate, and Kelly kindly showed me the best way to look major league. Shining up the baseball shoes is a passion at CDP.

It seems that there is a small corner of the umpiring world that is part of a "baseball snobbery." There is a hesitation to keep secrets within, and they don't share much. That's a minority thank goodness.

During the summer of 2019 that snobbery showed its ugly face to Kelly when he was crew chief. A small-minded member of his umpiring crew either obtained or filmed a snippet of video showing Kelly appearing to be out of position on the field. Kelly was indeed upset and all of us in Bunkhouse 41 came to his rescue.

Throughout many contacts with Kelly, there isn't a better man wearing the mask on the baseball field. I hope he's back!

26
The Coaches

BRYAN BRUNSWELL, ADAM Kern, Jim Kraut, and Jacob Russ are four incredible men who perhaps got less sleep than any of us umpires.

They are the head coaches of the teams from Pittsburgh, two from Michigan, and from Lake Norman, North Carolina who sponsored me. They stay in bunkhouses with the boys.

My advice to each one of them when I visited the players bunkhouse on their first night in camp? Get plenty of sleep and try to settle down in the bunkhouse.

The Dogs from Michigan were especially spirited, and Dan Pydyn was a parent and assistant coach. His team invited me to a sweet campsite where the parents were staying alongside a pool and with air-conditioned cabins.

Bryan Brunswell is a creative man and a musician, and he needed all his skills with his talented Pittsburgh team.

Typical of all the coaches, Kern from Clarkston, Michigan went to his two children and greeted them warmly after a loss. That was a good moment.

His team had been defeated and they all gathered with their opponents and kneeled around the mound to say thank you to God and to everyone for giving them so much.

That was an even greater moment.

All four of my teams were very competitive but did not make the final eight.

Amber Darbutt was the right-hand women who made it happen for the North Carolina team. It's a big business getting a team to Cooperstown.

27
Uncle Charlie

THE ONE PIECE of advice I always give to my coaches from teams who graciously sponsor me prior to coming to Cooperstown, is bring plenty of pitchers.

And make sure they know Uncle Charlie! That old-time baseball phrase is the description of a breaking ball, a curve ball. I know about Uncle Charlie, and recently was reminded of the lore by an old-time pitcher and lifelong friend, Ken Ollish from Pataskala, Ohio.

In the winter of 1967, while playing our brand of rough-house, outdoor basketball at Paul Obuchowski's house on South Street in Bellows Falls, Vermont, I put my right hand through a window. The driveway was narrow, and a garage was under the hoop. I came down from a layup, found myself knocked off balance, and put my hand out. Right into glass!

The cuts, once healed, turned out to be a great blessing when it came time to throwing a baseball. My right index finger, and my middle finger, to this day have deep scars.

It didn't take long to figure out that I could place the two scars directly over the seams of a baseball. The result, in today's baseball lingo, was filthy. I like to joke occasionally and enamor the story just a little bit. The ball would come out of my hand, go around the third baseman, and break all the way around to the strike zone.

I can still see my old pal Dick Long, in frustration, pounding his bat on the ground after my curve ball struck him out in Little League play. In a small town in Vermont (population 5,300) he played for the Elks and I played for the Rotary club. Since then he's been an umpire in Vermont.

So, when coaches prepare for Cooperstown's great tournament, no matter how fast a pitcher is, sooner or later he's going to get timed up by batters. The result? Typically, the batter hits a home run. Bring on Uncle Charlie.

28
Confidence Supreme

BRANDON HOWES IS the epitome of Mr. Baseball. He loved his first time in Cooperstown so much that he visited the Hall of Fame *four times* in a week.

He grew up on the West Coast and was a big fan of the late Tony Gwynn and the San Diego Padres.

He and Todd Guinther, from Pennslvania, were good buddies who hung out with me after games at the Upstate Restaurant. We talked baseball endlessly.

Brandon just looks like an umpire, tall and with trimmed chin whiskers. He was selected to a Final Four game his first week in Cooperstown.

Confidence is something we talked about often. Sometimes we are not so sure off the field with marriages and relationships, but the exact opposite on the diamond.

The same is true for Todd. When he did not get selected for the final night of action in the tournament, he was bummed. But that didn't make him any less of an umpire.

Todd told us positive stories about his love of Gettysburg in Pennsylvania. He's a gifted photographer, too.

Brandon loved those stories, too, but sooner or later the conversation turned to baseball and the hundreds of calls and decisions we make each game.

We decided that confidence is the number one ingredient to bring to each pitch, each inning and every game.

29
A Blast from the Past

A SPECIAL OCCASION in 2019 was a blast from my past. The 1981 Cooperstown High baseball team was a championship team, on and off the field.

Eight of them were waiting for me in July of 2019 at teammate Rich Busse's Pioneer Patio restaurant.

It was a mini reunion on Friday evening, my one day off from CDP umpiring duties.

Leader of the gang was Adam Hurtebise, he too, a writer. They all recognized me, but I initially did not recognize them. Most of them now have beards and slight bellies.

There was coach Mark Rathbone, looking like David Lettermen. He was so brave to allow me, in 1981 as sports editor of the Daily Star newspaper, to report on the team from the dugout in fabled Doubleday Field.

Next up from his seat to warmly greet me was Jim Curtis. A favorite player of many athletes I covered throughout the years he was all smiles as we robustly shook hands. "It's been, what, about 38 or 39 years, since we last got together?" he asked me.

He was in the dugout in 1981 at Doubleday Field and calmly made a bold prediction to me. The state playoffs for the 21-0 team were underway. He was going to the plate to hit a home run! And you know what, he did.

Hurtebise was the batboy for the team, and we talked with glee about the Doubleday homers hit by Curtis and by Busse.

Hurtebise is depicted in a 1981 photo, walking out to the far, distant church over the leftfield fence, to fetch a home run ball. He's now a city administrator in Massachusetts.

That was an unforgettable team and each individual soared high in their adult lives. I think it's the water in Cooperstown, and great parents like the late Bill Guilfoile who was the public relations director at the Hall of Fame.

Steve Smith and Eric Rudenber were the centerfielder and the catcher of the team and we lingered with Hurtebise for a long time talking. Both looked like they could still play.

Coach Henrici, Morley, Winters, Scott and Jim Curtis, Guilfoile, Feddermen, Schuermann, ah, the memories of such personalities came back so fresh.

The memories are now 40 years old.

They wanted to know if I still had the photo of actor Donald Sutherland attended by his attractive makeup person, and with Jim Curtis bedecked with a Phillies uniform in the background. Sutherland was in Cooperstown filming a movie at the time in legendary Doubleday Field.

The team members had noted the Cooperstown High photo, from 1981, was on my Facebook page. But they had a question. "Who was that makeup girl in the photo with Sutherland," Jim Curtis and the boys wanted to know.

The boys of Cooperstown.

30
A Homecoming

FATE IS AN amazing force of life. In 1979, I was invited to Oneonta-Cooperstown to interview for sports editor of the Ottaway Newspaper-owned Daily Star.

It was the best sports job of the 23-paper chain, back in the day when newspapers were the dominant media. Prior to going, sitting at the dining room table at my home in Bellows Falls, Vt., my parents, my grandmother and I haggled a bit just as a big snowstorm arrived.

My parents were worried about the journey. It was going to be an eight-hour drive with heavy snow on the road. It was if TV legend Burl Ives was there. Finally, my grandmother, who had suffered a stroke and never said much, spoke up.

"You would be a damn fool if you didn't go," she stated emphatically.

I went.

The publisher of the newspaper, the late Ed Somers, offered me the job and $250 per week. He also graciously arranged for me to be a lead reporter for the entire chain of papers for the upcoming 1980 Winter Olympic Games in Lake Placid, New York.

It was perhaps the best five years of my life.

I was married in 1982, bought my first house for $23,000, started my own business with the Sporting Eye weekly newspaper, and covered hundreds of major league and minor league baseball games, Division I football and soccer, and great hunting and fishing. I met so many fine people like the Art Bettiol family who essentially adopted this young writer from Vermont.

A horrific event happened in 1981 when covering a Cooperstown High Christmas basketball tournament. After hustling back 16 miles from Cooperstown to Oneonta, and in the middle of writing my story about legendary coach Dick White's team at 11 pm, I noticed somebody familiar coming in the backdoor. It was Jaclin Peper, a classy lady whom I would marry the following June. She had gut-wrenching news.

She told me my 21-year-old brother, Terry Brown, and Dana Fuller, had both died as volunteer firefighters battling a block fire in Bellows Falls.

Overall, the stunning reaction drove me into personal over drive and I resolved to honor Terry's memory by fiercely trying to be best at everything I did!

League players voted me MVP of the city basketball league in 1982, I played shortstop on an adult-league softball team, and founded and played in the Little Big Man Basketball Tournament.

But the best part of life was my role as sports editor was covering the National Baseball Hall of Fame in Cooperstown.

I had a one-on-one interview with Baseball Commissioner Bowie Kuhn, and attended the Otesaga Hotel's fabulous festivities, and a private luncheon for the Hall of Famers every year. Much of my connections were due in great part to a wonderful relationship with Bill Guilfoile, the late director of public relations at the HOF.

After perusing the wonderful luncheon spread with my parents in 1980, at the Otesaga, my father chattered like a youngster about the nice, short man, he had gone through the line together.

The short man was the tall legend, pitcher Warren Spahn.

My parents were there when I interviewed HOF pitcher Burleigh Grimes about his infamous spit ball, as many Hall of Famers were relaxing in the same rocking chairs that remain now on the lake overlooking Otesaga Lake.

Grimes of course denied, tongue in cheek, that he ever tossed a slippery elm pitch. My late mother was concerned that I was pestering the sage, old man.

Also, on the glamorous Otesaga hotel porch was Henry Aaron, Frank Robinson, and Bob Gibson. I interviewed all of them. But my favorite Hall of Famer was Cool Papa Bell of the old Negro Leagues.

A HOMECOMING

He was so fast that he could snap off the lights and be back in bed before it got dark.

Ted Williams, with a home at the time in Westminster, Vermont, gave me an autograph in 1980 and I have it framed today with an intimate photo I took of the Splendid Splinter.

The legendary Joe DiMaggio signed a front copy of my Sporting Eye newspaper, with his photo from the year before on the cover. He did not sign many autographs back in the day.

Hired by the New York Yankees to write a regular column for *Yankees* magazine, I was censored once by owner George Steinbrenner. He did not agree with me when I wrote that Don Mattingly, who had hit no less that .326 in five years in the minors, including Oneonta, would be a great Yankee.

Never losing sight of the magic of local sports, I played goalie against the champion girls field hockey team from Cooperstown High. We lost 10-1. Then, I covered Milford, just down the road from Cooperstown, when the tiny high school team won a championship. My photo that day depicts a giant man who was the coach, being carried off the field by seven elated, but struggling players.

Doubleday Field was a gem. It was 1939 when Babe Ruth, Cy Young and Ty Cobb sat at Doubleday Field for a portrait photograph. In the early 1980s, I was fortunate to be sitting in the Doubleday press box next to New York Times columnist George Vecsey when Willie Stargell belted an epic homer with the Pittsburgh Pirates. Later, Vecsey pulled out some notes the Boston Red Sox came one year, saying to watch in the later innings. The Red Sox had called up a big kid from Texas, and if this pitcher recovered from arm injuries, he could be pretty good. He was Roger Clemons.

John Elway was a shining star in the summer of 1982 not for his football exploits but for what he did for minor league baseball in Oneonta. He was a terrific right fielder, and I can close my eyes, and see Number 7 rifle the ball 400-feet, on a line, to the plate. The $160,000 that Steinbrenner paid him that summer in the NY Penn League, when he hit .301, was not enough to change his mind.

31
What do Umpires Talk About?

THE UMPIRES TALK about everything, and I mean everything, at the bunkhouses in between games.

Most umpires work about three games per day and resting and talking at the bunkhouse is a daily routine.

Unlike the many books about major league players, throughout the decades, the umpires never had a fight that I know of all summer. They don't drink inside the park; no alcohol is allowed at any time.

There were a few rough edges because a high percentage of the men are Donald Trump supporters. I'm a Republican but personally can't stand Trump's deceptive personality and long history of not telling the truth. We tried not to talk about him.

What do they talk about in the few hours and minutes between games and official events?

The list is long. Umpire signals that vary, wives, girlfriends, hunting, fishing, injuries, robots, replaying the game they just worked; at the top of the list is pay.

Not one single umpire of about 150 men, and a few female umpires that I met over four weeks, does the job, that most people won't do, for only money. But integrity and fair play is in order.

There is more and more pressure from coaches, players and fans at every game.

Here in Ohio, about 60 percent of all umpires quit after two years and unruly parents are cited as reasons why. Next up is the low pay. Officials in 2019 around the nation were threatened with their lives numerous times. Did you hear about the basketball referee in Ohio who was head-butted by an enraged parent? It was a sixth- grade team playing.

We talk between games about how many times we take a hit from

WHAT DO UMPIRES TALK ABOUT?

foul balls and even with the best equipment that costs over $1,000, can't protect every inch of an umpire.

Medics were called during one game that I was behind the plate in Cooperstown; a pitch somehow got past the catcher and hit me hard right in my left hand that was tucked behind the catcher's back.

I was bleeding profusely. It was taped up by the medic and the game went on. *That's the Cooperstown way.*

Some parents say the umpires are keeping their kid from getting a scholarship to college and of course making the majors soon after … Do these parents have any idea the odds are stacked up firm against their child? That's the only reason to play the sport?

Why do professionally trained umpires work for three hours, spend another two hours of travel and preparing (totaling five hours) and get paid in Ohio a flat fee of $42 or $55?

That's about $10 per hour. Travel ball is $50.

The dues, fees, and equipment cost at least $800 just to get started. Here in Ohio I took a loss on my umpiring in 2018 when all things like travel were not compensated.

We all are amazed at the disparity, and umpires talk about the need for solidarity and a uniform salary structure across the country. It seems a national or statewide union movement is warranted.

A common theme is umpire signals. It seems like each state has different standards on both pay and signals. Here in Ohio, some plate umpires kneel behind the plate and hardly ever leave that spot.

Other field umpires make the "hang five" signal, like here in Ohio, but most umpires haven't got a clue what this means.

So, do fans even recognize that umpires are talking silently to each other?

From California, the colorful Juarez brothers signal out calls by placing their righthand, stationary, over their hearts. Other umpires punch out runners with a quick jab. I like the windmill call on very close plays in the infield.

At the plate, some umps point to their right to signal a strike. I like the old-fashioned way of punching in front with my right fist.

THE UMPIRE'S BUNKHOUSE

All the umpires strive for consistency, fair play and balance on the field. But off the field, they are as different as you can imagine.

From Alabama, Bill Ward is animated and as OCD as a man can get. He is a perfect umpire, and he was selected to do the plate in the honored championship game. He can talk a mile a minute and he was very helpful to me.

In stark contrast to Ward, Reynaldo Cochrum is tall, quiet, and is a professional umpire. He was in our bunkhouse for only a week. He doesn't talk very much, and meticulously cares for his clothes.

Conclusion

Far more than muscle memory, and the rules of the illustrious game of baseball pounded into my brain, the memories of so many fine umpires and their stories were inspiring.

It was a blessing that so many fellow umpires, from every corner of the nation, helped rescued me from the bully.

It was an enriching experience, one of the sweetest of my life, being at Dreams Park for four weeks. Even staying in the primitive bunkhouse.

Don't holler at your umpire is a public program I now offer to schools, churches, civic organizations and as fund raisers. It is a celebration of 60 years of loving baseball. Contact me via email at Mikebrown552017@gmail.com.

Laugh, cry, think, and remember when.

Do you know who the greatest defensive right fielder in the history of professional baseball was? If you were around baseball, in Oneonta, NY in 1982, you know the answer.

God bless the umpires. Do not holler at them, ***please***.

Perhaps they slept the night before on a thin mattress, somebody kept them awake all night with snoring, and there was no air conditioning.

The man or woman behind the black mask is your friend not your foe. Oh, yes, umpires are supposedly perfect. They are not. But they are better than robots.

They are an interesting, rare breed of humans.

Maybe the last of the breed?

CPSIA information can be obtained
at www.ICGtesting.com
Printed in the USA
FSHW010003080620
70936FS